Ten P
about

ex libris

Candlestick Press

Published by:
Candlestick Press,
Diversity House, 72 Nottingham Road, Arnold, Nottingham NG5 6LF
www.candlestickpress.co.uk

Design and typesetting by Craig Twigg

Printed by Ratcliff & Roper Print Group, Nottinghamshire, UK

Selection and Introduction © Katharine Towers 2019

Cover illustration © Richard Shimell, 2019
www.richardshimell.co.uk

Candlestick Press monogram © Barbara Shaw, 2008

© Candlestick Press, 2019
Reprinted 2020

Donation to Woodland Trust
www.woodlandtrust.org.uk

ISBN 978 1 907598 78 4

Dedicated to the memory of Alistair Elliot (1932 – 2018) who loved trees.

Acknowledgements:

The poems in this pamphlet are reprinted from the following books, all by
permission of the publishers listed unless stated otherwise. Every effort has
been made to trace the copyright holders of the poems published in this book.
The editor and publisher apologise if any material has been included without
permission or without the appropriate acknowledgement, and would be glad
to be told of anyone who has not been consulted.

Thanks are due to all the copyright holders cited below for their kind
permission:

Moniza Alvi, *Europa* (Bloodaxe Books, 2008) www.bloodaxebooks.com.
Paul Batchelor, *The Sinking Road* (Bloodaxe Books, 2008)
www.bloodaxebooks.com. David Constantine, *Collected Poems* (Bloodaxe
Books, 2004) www.bloodaxebooks.com. Alistair Elliot, *Imaginary Lines*
(Shoestring Press, 2012) by kind permission of the Estate of Alistair Elliot
and Shoestring Press. Kim Moore, *The Art of Falling* (Seren Books, 2015).
Louisa Rhodes, *Wild Poetry* (Hive South Yorkshire, 2017) by kind permission
of the author. Ruby Robinson, *Every Little Sound* (Liverpool University
Press, 2016) by permission of PLS Clear.

All permissions cleared courtesy of Swift Permissions
(swiftpermissions@gmail.com).

Where poets are no longer living, their dates are given.

Introduction

John Clare said: "I felt it happiness to be / Unknown, obscure and like a tree." In fact, I'm not sure that trees are as obscure as he imagined. They line up on horizons and gather in parks and by rivers, their stateliness commanding our attention and respect, and reminding us of the briefness of our own lives. They also remind us of different kinds of art; in winter they are sculptures, in summer something more like music.

These ten poems are only a small offering from the vast forest of poems about trees. I am aware of omitting one or two canonical examples (such as Housman's loveliest cherry) but was motivated by a desire to introduce some lesser known poems and to encourage readers to venture off the beaten track.

The starting point for our little arboretum is DH Lawrence's rhapsodic celebration of the colours of the trees in his garden. Green overrides all, but his darting poet's eye notices the pinks and the whites and the blues, and the elder's graceful 'foam'. Elsewhere, we encounter an errant soul escaped from a fallen tree and carried off into the world inside a human body, or we shin up a trunk and don't want to come down. For Edward Thomas, looking at aspens shivering in the breeze is almost to become a tree himself.

Of course, we must acknowledge that we are losing our trees – to diseases such as ash die-back or to urban sprawl and inner city husbandry. Gerard Manley Hopkins' poem 'Binsey Poplars' stands for every lament for a lost tree, just as Alistair Elliot's elegiac 'Dear Betula' speaks for all those who love trees and hope never to be parted from them.

Katharine Towers

Trees in the Garden

Ah in the thunder air
how still the trees are!

And the lime-tree, lovely and tall, every leaf silent,
hardly looses even a last breath of perfume.

And the ghostly, creamy coloured little tree of leaves,
white, ivory white among the rambling greens,
how evanescent, variegated elder, she hesitates on the green grass
as if, in another moment, she would disappear
with all her grace of foam!

And the larch that is only a column, it goes up too tall to see:
and the balsam-pines that are blue with the gray-blue blueness of
things from the sea,
and the young copper beech, its leaves red-rosey at the ends,
how still they are together, they stand so still
in the thunder air, all strangers to one another
as the green grass glows upwards, strangers in the garden.

Lichtental.

DH Lawrence (1885 – 1930)

The Trees Outside My Window
(after Jules Supervielle)

I'm thankful to the trees outside my window.
Only they can reach into the depth of me.
Without them, I should have died long ago –
they keep my heart alive, its eager ways.

In the long willow branches, the dark cypress,
my own ghost hides, stares out at me,
knowing me so well, pitying me in this world.
So little understanding why I stay and stay.

Moniza Alvi

Binsey Poplars
felled 1879

My aspens dear, whose airy cages quelled,
Quelled or quenched in leaves the leaping sun,
All felled, felled, are all felled;
    Of a fresh and following folded rank
        Not spared, not one
        That dandled a sandalled
      Shadow that swam or sank
On meadow and river and wind-wandering weed-winding bank.

O if we but knew what we do
        When we delve or hew —
    Hack and rack the growing green!
       Since country is so tender
    To touch, her being só slender,
    That, like this sleek and seeing ball
    But a prick will make no eye at all,
      Where we, even where we mean
         To mend her we end her,
      When we hew or delve:
After-comers cannot guess the beauty been.
    Ten or twelve, only ten or twelve
      Strokes of havoc únselve
        The sweet especial scene,
      Rural scene, a rural scene,
      Sweet especial rural scene.

Gerard Manley Hopkins (1844 – 1889)

The Dead Tree

How easy it is to love the dead tree,
despite not knowing its kind,
its branches spread against the sky.
Even in death it reaches upward,
before the left hand turn,
after the shortcut across the moor.
In winter, in the fog,
sheep lie on the road for warmth
until the car is close enough
to breathe on them
and then they straighten their legs
and clatter away like coat hangers.
It's easy to think that nobody
has been this way for years.
This is the right time, eight
or nine at night. The workers
from Sellafield already home,
they have forgotten the sea
and the beach of stones
in the bright light of home.
Today, someone has left a mattress
miles from the nearest town,
on the corner of the switchback,
half-folded on its side,
a woman posing for a painting.
A farmer raises one index finger
less than half an inch
to acknowledge you,
mistaking you for someone
who belongs here,
because of the time of night,
because you don't use your brakes
to slow the car down, just
the natural camber of the road,
he doesn't know you're only
here for the tree, he'd think you mad

but how many things does he know
that never change, shouldn't this be
a tourist spot with a myth of its own:
Here is the tree, struck by lightning
five terrible times and it survived
until the last, when it dropped
every leaf it had and would ever have
down to the ground in fright.
Maybe some part of it fell like he did
and its soul jumped from its wood and fled
and its trunk and each branch
turned white in shock,
but its poor tree soul, only used
to moving in the wind or hunching
its shoulders against rain or snow,
so used to being tree-shaped,
feeling rooted all through the earth,
the tree soul couldn't find its way back
so it jumped into the nearest living thing.
Someone is changing their mind
with the seasons, someone is losing
everything then finding it again.
Somebody is walking around
with a tree soul inside them.

Kim Moore

Yew Tree

(Botanical name: taxus baccata)

They have come to mourn again.
I find it strange.
Sometimes they cry and hold hands,
rub each other's backs as if
the warmth will banish
the cold. It makes me sad
to see them so empty,
so disregarding of the kind flowers
and birds that come to keep them
company. Sometimes they just stand still
and apart, untouching, like trees
on a windless day.

Louisa Rhodes

Aspens

All day and night, save winter, every weather,
Above the inn, the smithy, and the shop,
The aspens at the cross-roads talk together
Of rain, until their last leaves fall from the top.

Out of the blacksmith's cavern comes the ringing
Of hammer, shoe, and anvil; out of the inn
The clink, the hum, the roar, the random singing –
The sounds that for these fifty years have been.

The whisper of the aspens is not drowned,
And over lightless pane and footless road,
Empty as sky, with every other sound
Not ceasing, calls their ghosts from their abode,

A silent smithy, a silent inn, nor fails
In the bare moonlight or the thick-furred gloom,
In tempest or the night of nightingales,
To turn the cross-roads to a ghostly room.

And it would be the same were no house near.
Over all sorts of weather, men, and times,
Aspens must shake their leaves and men may hear
But need not listen, more than to my rhymes.

Whatever wind blows, while they and I have leaves
We cannot other than an aspen be
That ceaselessly, unreasonably grieves,
Or so men think who like a different tree.

Edward Thomas (1878 – 1917)

Tree Climbing

Grasp this: it doesn't matter if the rasp
of bark to palm is second nature or
if this is your first time, there are

no experts: ash or oak, the look of bole
or canopy means nothing till you throw
yourself off balance, wrap

your feet around the branch you hold
and from that new perspective see
how the world hangs: head over heels

it all floods back to a heart
that won't forget vertigo's bloodrush
nor come down when they call.

Paul Batchelor

The Apple Tree

Night gone and the dream is stranded
Or this is a bold dream that has stepped some paces forward
The apple tree in a startling frost

Faces the sun in a clothing from elsewhere
Crackles with a freezing fire. There are no proofs
Only these goadings. The frost

Rasped like a cat's tongue at the windowpanes.
She entered suddenly with all her clothes in a bundle
Backing the door to throw the bundle down.

Waking I remember the ha'pennies
I warmed as a child and laid against the frost
To see. I watch the bright grey apple tree

Slowly denuding, slowly vanishing.

David Constantine

Undress

There is an ash tree behind this house. You
can see it from our bedroom window.
If you stare at it for long enough, you'll see
it drop a leaf. Stare at it now, you said,
and notice the moment a leaf strips away
from its branch, giving a twirl. Consider this.

The ash tree unclothes itself Octoberly.
From beside our bed, fingering the curtain,
observe the dark candles at the top of
that tree, naked and alert, tending to the breeze.
A sheet of ice between the rooftops
and this noiseless sky has turned the air

inside out. Black veins of branches
shake against the blue screen on which they
hang. Small mammals are hibernating
in pellets of warm air under ground. But,
in spite of the cold, this ash tree does not shy
from shrugging off its coat, sloping its nude

shoulders to the night. So, you said, undo,
unbutton, unclasp, slowly remove. Let down your
hair, breathe out. Stand stark in this room until
we remember how not to feel the chill.
Stand at the window, lift your arms right up
like a tree. Yes – like that. Watch leaves drop.

Ruby Robinson

Dear Betula

Loveliest of trees, when I am dead
I'll get up from my dirty bed
To watch you wave your delicate hair
At every passing train of air.

A lifetime's watching was too short
For human lovers to pay court
To you, but I shall make amends
After my little lifetime ends.

I shall be in that passing train,
A waving ghost, as you remain
Trembling more beautifully still
And waving back as well, until
You also cease ... to be a tree ...
And cross that boundary, to me.

Alistair Elliot (1932 – 2018)